A BLUE BANNER BIOGRAPHY

Jodie Foster

By John Bankston

P.O. Box 196
Hockessin, Delaware 19707
Visit us on the web: www.mitchelllane.com
Comments? email us: mitchelllane@mitchelllane.com

Printing   1   2   3   4   5   6   7   8   9

Blue Banner Biographies

Eminem	Sally Field	**Jodie Foster**
Melissa Gilbert	Rudy Giuliani	Ron Howard
Michael Jackson	Jennifer Lopez	Nelly
Mary-Kate and Ashley Olsen	Daniel Radcliffe	Selena
Shirley Temple	Richie Valens	Rita Williams-Garcia

Library of Congress Cataloging-in-Publication Data
Bankston, John, 1974-
        Jodie Foster / John Bankston
              p. cm. -- (A blue banner biography.)
        Includes index.
        Filmography: p.
        Summary: A biography of the Academy Award winning actress, Jodie Foster, from her work as a child in advertisements through her motion picture successes and failures.
        ISBN 1-58415-171-4 (lib. bdg.)
            1. Foster, Jodie—Juvenile literature. 2. Motion picture actors and actresses—United States—Biography—Juvenile literature. [1. Foster, Jodie. 2. Actors and actresses. 3. Women—Biography.] I. Title II. Series
PN2287.F624 B36 2002
791. 43′028′092--dc21
                                                2002008321

ABOUT THE AUTHOR: Born in Boston, Massachussetts, **John Bankston** began publishing articles in newspapers and magazines while still a teenager. Since then, he has written over two hundred articles, and contributed chapters to books such as *Crimes of Passion,* and *Death Row 2000,* which have been sold in bookstores across the world. He has written numerous biographies for young adults, including *Mandy Moore* and *Alexander Fleming and the Story of Penicillin* (Mitchell Lane). He currently lives in Portland, Oregon.

PHOTO CREDITS: Cover: The Kobal Collection; p. 4 Donald Sanders/Globe Photos; p. 8 Foster/Wagener/Shooting Star; p. 13 The Kobal Collection; p. 15 Getty Images; p. 18 Globe Photos; p. 21 The Kobal Collection/Paramount; p. 24 Associated Press; p. 27 Sportsphoto Ltd./Allstar

CONTENTS

Jodie Foster, shown here as a teenager. Jodie has been a star from the age of three, and continues her acting career today.

Discovered

Brandy Foster had a secret. She carried the secret with her as she endured separation, then divorce from her husband, Lucius Foster. Getting a divorce in early 1960's California was fairly difficult, but as she went through the legal proceedings, Brandy kept the secret to herself.

She was pregnant.

She decided not to tell her soon to be ex-husband. After all, what was the point? The couple already had two daughters and a son and Lucius's inability to support them was a big reason for the divorce. Brandy didn't think their father, called "a dreamer" by some, "a con-man" by others, but "charming" by nearly everyone he met, was going to change. Brandy Foster was on her way to being a single mother.

By the time Alicia Christian Foster was born on November 19, 1962 in Los Angeles, California, her mother Brandy was divorced. Being a single mom in the early

1960s was even more challenging than it is today. Women in the workforce encountered greater discrimination, and the children of such families endured more stigmas. Because she had little education and lacked much in the way of job training, Brandy faced great obstacles.

Brandy was a nickname Evelyn Foster was given as a little girl; Brandy passed that tradition on to her daughter. Alicia Christian was the name chosen by her ex-husband's family, but Brandy called her baby girl Jodie.

Back when girls were still expected to be ladylike, Jodie was the perfect name for a tomboy.

Years later, a teenage Jodie would tell an interviewer, "Those are the names the family wanted, but when my mother got me home from the hospital, she hated them, so she always called me Jodie. If anyone called me by those names now to aggravate me, I'd hit 'em."

The name fit. Nearly 40 years ago, Alicia might have seemed too girlish a name for a kid who played rough, enjoyed sports with the boys and was more comfortable in jeans than skirts. Back when girls were still expected to be ladylike, Jodie was the perfect name for a tomboy.

For Brandy and her children, money was a major problem. Lucius Foster, the children's father, had been ordered by the courts to pay $600 a month in child support, but he rarely did. Brandy worked part time as a film publicist for a producer to earn money, but hated leaving her children for long hours. There had to be another option.

The mother was blessed with a tight circle of female friends, most of them divorced, some of them struggling. She asked them about getting her kids into show business.

Hollywood is the place where people break into movies, television, and commercials. It is one of the few ways a kid in grade school can earn more money than his or her parents.

Brandy thought Jodie's older brother Buddy would be perfect for commercials and her friends agreed. One of them introduced her to an agent, a person whose job is finding actors work and who earns a percentage of his or her clients' salaries.

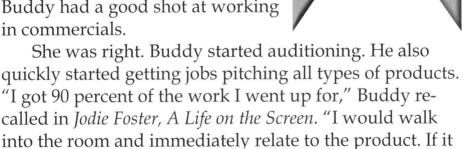

Jodie's mom Brandy thought Jodie's older brother Buddy would be perfect for commercials.

Toni Kelman was just getting started. Her office was a converted garage. Despite outward appearances, Brandy had a good feeling about Toni. The agent thought Buddy had a good shot at working in commercials.

She was right. Buddy started auditioning. He also quickly started getting jobs pitching all types of products. "I got 90 percent of the work I went up for," Buddy recalled in *Jodie Foster, A Life on the Screen.* "I would walk into the room and immediately relate to the product. If it was a toy, my eyes would light up and I was excited

Jodie (front) is shown here in 1963 with her brother Buddy (left).

about it. My first ad was for Kellogg's Corn Flakes and I told them I loved the cereal." After a couple of years, he also began landing acting roles, getting parts on *Green Acres* and *Hondo*. Eventually, he earned a role on *Mayberry R.F.D*, a wholesome program about rural life, where he played the son of the show's lead. It lasted four years, and made Buddy a star. He got piles of fan mail and was recognized when he went out with his family. By the time he was 10, Buddy was earning over $25,000 a year—more than most working adults in the early 1970s.

Buddy also helped Jodie get her big break.

When he was five years old, Buddy got an interview for Coppertone suntan lotion. Although Buddy had Toni as his agent, Brandy acted as his manager, handling his money and making sure he got to his auditions on time. Jodie was only three years old; Brandy was not about to let the toddler wait out in the car!

She came in with her mother and older brother, waiting in the room while Buddy met with casting executives. With his pale, freckled skin, they were not sure if he was right for the job. Then, they noticed his sister.

Like lots of little sisters, Jodie looked up to her older brother and often imitated him. While Buddy auditioned for the job, Jodie stood right behind him, posing, flexing her muscles, and giggling. The blue-eyed, blonde-haired little girl who seemed the perfect image of a California child charmed the executives. They huddled for a few minutes before coming to a quick decision. The ad's star would no longer be a boy, but a girl: Jodie Foster.

Jodie came in with her mother and older brother for her brother's interview with Coppertone suntan lotion.

The Coppertone ad was set on the beach with a family having fun in the sun. Interestingly, soon after the ad was televised, a print ad for Coppertone was released, featuring "Little Miss Coppertone" at the beach with a dog pulling at her swimsuit bottoms. Because the ad was released so soon after Jodie's television ad, it was commonly thought that Jodie was Little Miss Coppertone. In reality, the model for Little Miss Coppertone was the ad artist's daughter.

Though Jodie had nothing to do with the print ad, a little luck and being in the right place at the right time launched Jodie's career.

Kid Parts

*J*odie did commercial after commercial. By the time she was eight, she had appeared in over three dozen ads and earned guest parts ranging from her debut on brother Buddy's show to an appearance on *Sesame Street*. The adults who worked with young Jodie could not believe how professional she was. At five years old Jodie could read a script, and when she arrived on a set she knew her lines. She always hit her mark by standing on the pieces of tape on the floor indicating where she needed to be, and she never threw tantrums.

Brandy moved the family first to Newport Beach, a coastal community in Orange County and later to Los Angeles when the long drive to Jodie's jobs and auditions became too much. The tiny bungalow in a seedy part of Hollywood may not have been an ideal home, but as Jodie remembers, her mother fixed it up to resemble an Italian villa. It was a "pretty normal American family existence," Jodie explained in *Biography* magazine, but her mother did things to offer her children views of other cultures, despite their uneven money. She took them to museums and inexpensive showings of art films. "European films were her passion. She loved Europe and she dreamed of going there. The films she took me to became my touchstones as a child," Jodie remembered.

Brandy's love for European culture, particularly French culture, was one reason she enrolled Jodie in College Lycée Français, an exclusive Los Angeles private school where students were taught in French. Many of its children were the offspring of movie stars and Hollywood production executives, but between Jodie and Buddy's earnings, Brandy had enough saved to pay the tuition. Jodie was eight years old when she began attending classes. She was also working regularly.

That year Brandy made two decisions that Toni disagreed with. First, Brandy decided not to let Jodie do any more commercials. Her daughter's face seemed to be on TV all the time, and she did not want Jodie becoming overexposed.

Her second choice seemed even more outrageous. Jodie would not work for scale, which is the set amount of money that actors who guest star on TV shows get

> *Jodie's mother decided that Jodie would no longer appear in commercials, and would only act in films and television shows.*

paid. Instead of earning the standard $450 a week, Brandy asked that Jodie be paid $1,000.

With those demands, Toni wondered if Jodie would ever work again. She did not have to wonder long. Jodie was a polished and professional actress, and even at her new asking price, producers lined up to hire her. Jodie continued to do guest appearances on TV shows earning a recurring role in the popular *Courtship of Eddie's Father* as a motherless child, and a voiceover on *The Addams Family*.

After her audition for another TV show, *Kung Fu*, the program's director, John Badham, told his wife, "You're not going to believe this, but I've got a crush on a ten year old girl." Jodie would go on to guest on the show, and Badham, who would later direct the films *Wargames* and *Saturday Night Fever*, explained in the biography *Jodie*, "It was just that inexplicable thing called 'presence'... She was just right there, just whatever was needed... You felt like you were in the presence of an adult."

> **Even at Jodie's new asking price, producers lined up to hire the polished and professional actress.**

Despite the tough kid roles and an almost adult way of acting, Jodie was a good fit for Disney.

Famous for its animated movies, the film studio produced dozens of live action pictures in the 1960s and

1970s. They were modestly budgeted films where kids were smart and heroic just like Jodie Foster.

She landed the part in *Napoleon and Samantha*, a movie about a young girl and her best friend who run away with a circus lion and stay with a recluse, played by actor Michael Douglas. Shot on location in Oregon, it meant Brandy and Jodie would have to leave the rest of the family in Los Angeles, where Jodie's older sisters Lucinda and Constance looked out for Buddy.

One potentially serious incident happened on the set of *Napoleon and Samantha* when no one seemed to be looking out for Jodie. It was late in the afternoon and hot. The

Jodie was bitten by the lion she worked with in Napoleon and Samantha. *The regular toothless lion was not behaving, so a lion with teeth was substituted for the regular lion.*

regular lion, a toothless beast named Major, refused to work.

The crew brought in Zambo, a stand-in who had all of his teeth. "Finally we got the shot," Jodie told artist Andy Warhol in his *Interview* magazine. "I was walking up the hill and the lion was behind me, being pulled by piano wire—that was the only way they could get him to go. And I wasn't walking fast enough. He came around and bit me."

The lion tamer saved her and Jodie was rushed to a Portland hospital. Although the bite was not too deep, she endured 17 shots as a precaution against rabies. Nearly two weeks later, Jodie was given the choice to go back to the movie or quit. "My mom left it up to me," she explained in *Interview*, "but I think it was smarter to go back, you know, get back on the horse that bucked me."

After surviving a lion attack, the plucky kid figured she had what it took to be an actress. Disney agreed, and the studio cast her in *One Little Indian* and a musical version of *Tom Sawyer*, where she played Becky Thatcher. In *Newsday*, a reviewer said, "her vocal intonations [singing] and facial expressions are charming—but it's the charm of someone two to three times her actual age of nine."

That was part of Jodie's problem.

> *After surviving a lion attack, Jodie figured she had what it took to be an actress.*

She continued to guest on TV shows, and landed a regular part on *Paper Moon*, which was based on the hit movie. The show was scheduled opposite the hugely popular *The Waltons* and was cancelled after a year. Unfortunately, none of Jodie's work on the big screen seemed destined to bring her fame and fortune.

"There wasn't a lot of depth to my roles," Jodie complained in *Biography* magazine. "Just kid parts in kid movies."

All of that changed after Jodie Foster auditioned for Martin Scorsese.

Iris

Martin Scorsese was part of a new generation of Hollywood filmmakers who transformed cinema. Like his peers, Scorsese, a New York University film school grad, crafted movies that were dark, edgy and real. He got his start directing the low budget exploitation picture, *Boxcar Bertha*, then gained fame for *Mean Streets*. Jodie Foster and her mother saw it four times before she met Martin. She was auditioning for the part of Audrey in his next movie, *Alice Doesn't Live Here Anymore*.

"In comes this little girl with a Lauren Bacall voice," Martin recalled in *Time* magazine. "She cracked us up."

Jodie got the part. As a tough kid who befriends Alice's son Tommy, Jodie's part was small but memorable.

As Audrey, she played a young girl wise beyond her years, introducing herself to Tommy by asking, "You wanna get high on Ripple [cheap wine]?"

Although the role required much more of Jodie than a silly Disney movie, her part was filmed in only two days. This is an extraordinarily brief amount of time for such a complex performance. In a 1991 interview with *Premiere Magazine*, director Scorsese said, "If we had had a few more days with her we could have had some real fine improvisations. But the kid is a real pro…"

The largest issue arrived when the woman assigned by California to watch out for the young actors "came over to me and said, 'Stop,'" Scorsese recalled in the interview. "I said, 'What do you mean, stop?' She said, 'Stop. The kid has got to go to school.'"

So they stopped. Jodie's job on *Alice* was over and she was back to school. Still the way she handled such a small role made it seem like she could also handle the first big hurdle every child star faces: puberty.

Older brother Buddy was not so lucky. He grew into an awkward adolescent and found little work. He later said he felt "abandoned" by Brandy, whose energy was focused on Jodie's career. By age 18, Buddy was married, using drugs, and parking cars at the Beverly Hills Hotel after discovering that the trust fund he thought was waiting for him once he became an adult was empty. In 1997, Buddy published a revealing book called *Foster Child* that detailed his diffi-

In 1975, Jodie was hired for a part which would change her life twice.

cult childhood and revealed secrets about Jodie's life. Jodie would later describe Buddy in *Time* magazine as "a distant acquaintance motivated solely by greed and sour grapes."

In 1975, Martin Scorsese hired 13-year-old Jodie for a part which would change her life twice.

Taxi Driver was a movie about an angry loner named Travis Bickle (played by Robert DeNiro) as he drives his taxi through the mean streets of 1970s New York. When Betsy (played by Cybill Shepherd), a woman he likes, spurns him, he tries to assassinate the presidential candidate she works for. When that fails, he befriends Iris, a 12-

Jodie played a 12-year-old prostitute in the movie Taxi Driver. *The role gave her the opportunity to play a part with more depth than her previous roles.*

year-old prostitute, whom he later rescues from her pimp in the movie's violent, bloody climax.

Jodie was cast as Iris, the young prostitute. It was a role so controversial that it is still discussed today, nearly 30 years later.

But to Brandy, who read the script before Jodie did, it was an important, career changing part. Playing Iris, Jodie had to dress in revealing outfits, curse, and smoke. As a professional actress for a decade, and the family breadwinner, Jodie knew something about what it was like to be independent and an adult. She explained in an *US* magazine interview, "I wasn't playing a prostitute in *Taxi Driver*. I was playing a runaway."

> Jodie's role in *Taxi Driver* attracted the attention of an angry loner obsessed with the movie.

The performance was so powerful it earned her an Academy Award nomination in 1977 for Best Supporting Actress. It changed her life, transforming her into a movie star. The role also attracted the attention of a loner, very much like Travis Bickle, who would change her life a second time.

And while the first change brought her the kind of fame and fortune most actresses only dream of, the second left her craving the kind of privacy few movie stars ever receive.

The Loner

*J*odie Foster made the transition from kiddie parts to adult roles seamlessly, something Buddy and countless other child stars are unable to do. "People ask me, 'how did you do it?'… I haven't robbed any banks—yet," Jodie joked in *Biography* magazine. "I think it's a question of who you are and how you're raised and how you process the information. It's like being an astronaut: there are some people who can't take the thinness of the air and the loneliness and freak out the second you put them in the suit. And there are some people who just love it, who can't wait to get in the capsule. Some people are built for it, and some aren't. If you're not it can be enormously destructive."

As she hit her teen years, Jodie worked in a perfect balance of material. There were light comedic Disney flicks, like *Candleshoe* and *Freaky Friday*, where she played a teen who switches bodies with her mother. She starred in an all-kid, gangster musical, *Bugsy Malone*, where her 200 co-stars shared two huge dressing rooms, and she had a trailer all to herself.

The French-speaking Jodie translated for adults Martin Scorsese and Robert DeNiro at the Cannes Film Festival, then went on to appear in the racy French movies *Moi, Fluer Bleue* (*My Blue Flower* - released in the United States as *Stop Calling Me Baby!*) and *Casotto* (*The Beach*

Jodie in Bugsy Malone, *an all-kid gangster musical.*

House). She guest hosted *Saturday Night Live*—the youngest host ever to do so until Drew Barrymore in 1982. She played Rynn in *The Little Girl Who Lives Down the Lane* where she survived without parents and poisoned a child molester played by Martin Sheen. It was a performance every bit as gritty as the one she had turned in for Iris.

Jodie related to Rynn, who managed her own life, telling gossip columnist Marilyn Beck, "I'm treated as an adult now, and have been for a long time."

There were missteps. In *The Little Girl Who Lives Down the Lane*, Jodie walked off the set after the movie's producer kept pressuring her to do a nude scene. The scene was later doubled by her older sister Constance. When Brandy learned that Robert DeNiro needed a beautiful actress as his co-star for *Raging Bull*, she convinced 15-year-old Jodie to pose for risqué photos to prove she could handle the material. Robert felt Jodie looked too young for the role and the pictures surfaced years later much to Jodie's embarrassment.

> **For the most part, teenaged Jodie was doing a good job navigating the path to adult actress.**

Still, for the most part, teenaged Jodie was doing a good job navigating the path to adult actress. In *Carny*, playing a woman fought over by two men, Jodie at 17 took on a role written for an actress in her mid-20s. As Adrian Lyne, the director of *Foxes*, put it, "It was strange… You felt that she was more mature than her mother."

Foxes was the story of four girls, teens growing up too fast in Los Angeles' San Fernando Valley. Jodie starred as Jeanie, an intelligent but risk-taking 16 year old. "Are there any nice people left in the world?" Jeanie's mother, played by Sally Kellerman, asked her in the movie. "You're all like short 40 year olds and you're tough ones."

In real life, Jodie's toughness was about to get tested.

In 1980, she graduated first in her class of 30 at College Lycée Français. Jodie gave her valedictory speech in French. She had already made plans normal for many 18 year olds. She had received acceptance letters from Harvard, Columbia, Stanford and many other colleges, but chose Yale University, an Ivy League school in New Haven, Connecticut.

Twenty years ago when Jodie interrupted a promising acting career to go away to college, many in the industry thought she was crazy. But because of her choice, when an actress like Claire Danes makes the same decision, it is accepted and she is said to be "pulling a Jodie Foster."

At Yale, Jodie majored in English Literature, shared a dorm room with two other young women, smoked too

> *In 1980, Jodie graduated first in her class of 30 at College Lycée Français.*

John Hinckley, Jr. attempted to assassinate President Ronald Reagan in the hopes of impressing Jodie.

much, put on the freshman 15 (-pound) weight gain from pizza and junk food, and tried to forget that in the real world she had been a movie star.

The real world would not let her forget.

A man who had seen *Taxi Driver* 15 times and fallen in love with Jodie's character, ripped her from her cloistered New Haven world. He was a child of wealth, but a man whose own failures mirrored Travis Bickle's and became just as overwhelming.

His name was John Hinckley, Jr. He sent Jodie fan letters and poems. He stalked her on campus. He even managed to call her, talking to her twice on the phone.

For Hinckley, that was not enough.

In *Taxi Driver*, Travis tried to get Betsy's attention by attempting to assassinate a presidential candidate.

In Washington, D.C., John tried to get Jodie's attention by attempting to assassinate a real-life president. On March 30, 1981, .22 caliber bullets from the 25-year-old Hinckley's gun wounded President Ronald Reagan and three other men, including his press secretary, who was permanently disabled in the attack.

John Hinckley, Jr.'s actions also changed Jodie's life forever. She left her dorm and only traveled the Yale campus with armed bodyguards. After a play that she was in attracted a Hinckley copycat, a man who was later arrested for a similar plot, Jodie gave up student theater.

Her French literature professor, Jacques Guicharnaud told *Biography* magazine, "I got the feeling she was a little lonely."

Other than a small press conference in 1981 and a piece she wrote for *Esquire* the next year, Jodie has refused to discuss the incident. But Hinckley's act, and its aftermath, forced Jodie to become a very private movie star.

> *After Hinckley shot Ronald Reagan in an attempt to impress Jodie, she became a very private movie star.*

Adult Star

By the time Jodie Foster graduated from Yale in May 1985, she had completed several movies, including *Mesmerized* and *The Hotel New Hampshire*. The work kept her from graduating in the standard four years, but it did not do much for her career.

After graduation, the one thing most critics said about films like *Siesta* and *Five Corners*, was that she was the best thing in them. Critically abused and ignored by audiences, these pictures, along with movies like *Stealing Home*, which did better with reviewers but still lost money, left people wondering if Jodie had finally succumbed to the child star curse.

Although the decade gave Jodie her first chance to direct for the TV show *Tales from the Dark Side* and to produce the movie *Mesmerized*, by 1987, the eighties looked like a wash.

"Women aren't allowed to make the same mistakes as men," she later complained to the *LA Times*. "Look at somebody like Michael Douglas. How many movies does he get to make that earn no money before he gets paid less money? And how long does it take an actress? One film that doesn't do well and you're back at square one."

Where Jodie wound up after her string of box office failures was on the set of a low budget movie shot in Canada. The producers did not even think she was right for the part. In the movie called *The Accused*, she played Sarah Tobias, a blue collar rape victim who is helped by prosecutor Kelly McGillis. Before it was released, gossip

Jodie Foster's acting career is just as successful today as it was when she was a child. She is shown here at the premiere of her 2002 movie Panic Room.

about the movie's co-stars earned more press than Jodie's acting.

Audiences then saw her performance.

As rape victim Sarah, Jodie was tough and vulnerable, sad and hopeful. She was *real*. Jodie's performance was a reminder to many audiences who had not seen her since *Taxi Driver* what a talented actress she was. No one was surprised when Jodie was nominated for an Academy Award again. This time she received the nomination for Best Actress in a Leading Role, and this time she won.

Jodie Foster won another Academy Award for Best Actress in a Leading Role for *The Silence of the Lambs*. She is the only woman to win two Oscars before turning 30.

Jodie has directed two movies and formed her own production company.

In the nearly 15 years since *The Accused*, Jodie has directed two movies, formed her own production company (Egg Pictures which closed in 2001), and appeared separately on numerous lists which named her as one of Hollywood's most powerful women and one of its most beautiful. Like her mother, Jodie has become a single mom, giving birth to sons Charles in 1998, and Kit in 2001. The identity of the father remains a guarded secret.

Many things about Jodie's life are kept private. "This is an American phenomenon," she told the *LA Times*, "that people think that they interact with a celebrity by hearing them talk about pain. So they think they know them."

Hollywood, and the gossip press that writes about it, seems to fill in spaces, areas about anyone's lives that are not discussed. Jodie keeps her private life private. She does not discuss her love life in interviews. Other celebrities do but she does not, and because not much is known about her private life, there is gossip. Despite what tabloids might report, or what rumors may be discussed, Jodie has never confirmed the gossip.

To those who suggest she should, they would do well to remember the acceptance speech she gave after winning an Oscar for *The Accused*. She thanked her mother Brandy, who "taught me that all my finger paintings were Picassos and that I didn't have to be afraid. And mostly that cruelty might be very human and it might be very cultural but it's *not acceptable*."

This is a lesson that Jodie Foster has taught in her work and her life as she has made the journey from child star to adult actress.

> **Despite Hollywood gossip, Jodie manages to keep her private life private.**

CHRONOLOGY

1962 Alicia Christian Foster is born on November 19, in Los Angeles, California.

1965 lands her first commercial, for Coppertone suntan lotion

1970 mother Brandy restricts Jodie from doing any more commercials, and limits her to TV shows and film.

1972 Debuts in Disney film, *Napoleon and Samantha.*

1980 graduates valedictorian from College Lycée Français in Los Angeles; delivers graduation speech in French.

1980 begins attending Yale University.

1981 John Hinckley, Jr. admits that his attempted assassination of President Ronald Reagan was done to impress Jodie. She begins attending classes with armed security guards.

1985 graduates from Yale Magna Cum Laude with a degree in literature.

1991 makes feature film directorial debut with *Little Man Tate.*

1994 forms production company Egg Pictures.

1997 brother Buddy publishes a tell-all book about Jodie, and she cuts off all contact with him.

1998 Jodie admits to being pregnant, but will not name the father; son Charles is born on July 20.

2001 Second son Kit is born on September 29; production company Egg Pictures shut down in part so she can spend more time with her sons.

2002 makes *People* magazine's 50 Most Beautiful People list

2003 completes voice over work for animated film *Tucker*

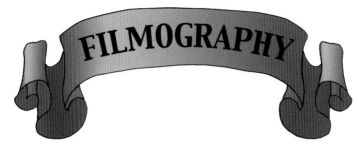

FILMOGRAPHY

1972	*Kansas City Bomber*
1972	*Napoleon and Samantha*
1973	*Tom Sawyer*
1973	*Rookie of the Year*
1973	*One Little Indian*
1974	*Alice Doesn't Live Here Anymore*
1974	*Smile Jenny, You're Dead*
1976	*Echoes of a Summer*
1976	*Taxi Driver*
1976	*Bugsy Malone*
1976	*The Little Girl Who Lives Down the Lane*
1976	*Freaky Friday*
1977	*Stop Calling Me Baby!*
1977	*Beach House*
1977	*Candleshoe*
1980	*Foxes*
1980	*Carny*
1982	*O'Hara's Wife*
1984	*The Blood of Others*
1984	*The Hotel New Hampshire*
1986	*Mesmerized*
1987	*Five Corners*
1987	*Siesta*
1988	*Stealing Home*
1988	*The Accused*
1989	*Catchfire*
1991	*The Silence of the Lambs*
1991	*Little Man Tate*
1992	*Shadows and Fog*
1993	*Sommersby*
1994	*Nell*

1994	*Maverick*
1997	*Contact*
1999	*Anna and the King*
2000	*Waking the Dead*
2002	*The Dangerous Lives of Altar Boys*
2002	*Panic Room*
2003	*Tucker*

As Director:

1984	*"Tales from the Darkside"* (TV Series)
1991	*Little Man Tate*
1995	*Home for the Holidays*
2003	*Flora Plum*

Television:

1968	*Mayberry R.F.D.*
1969	*The Courtship of Eddie's Father*
1969	*Sesame Street*
1970	*The Partridge Family*
1970	*Menace on the Mountain*
1972	*Kung Fu*
1973	*The Addams Family* (series)
1973	*Bob & Carol & Ted & Alice* (series)
1973	*Rookie of the Year*
1974	*Paper Moon* (series)
1975	*The Secret Life of T.K. Dearing*
1982	*Hollywood's Children*
1983	*Svengali*

FOR FURTHER READING

Books:

de Angelis, Therese. *Jodie Foster*. Philadelphia, PA: Chelsea House Publishers, 2000.

Foster, Buddy and Leon Wagener. *Foster Child: An Intimate Biography of Jodie Foster by Her Brother*. New York: Signet, 1998.

On the Web:

IMDb: Jodie Foster
    us.imdb.com/M/person-exact?Foster%2C%20Jodie

Jodie Foster at Thespian Net
    www.thespiannet.com/actresses/F/foster_jodie/index.shtml

INDEX

	DATE DUE		
OCT 08 2007			